Amazing Snakes
OF THE
Southwest
AND
West Coast

Parker Holmes

PowerKiDS press
New York

Published in 2015 by The Rosen Publishing Group, Inc.
29 East 21st Street, New York, NY 10010

First Edition

Editor: Jennifer Way
Book Design: Andrew Povolny
Photo Research: Katie Stryker

Photo Credits: Cover Tom Bean/The Image Bank/Getty Images; p. 5 TOM MCHUGH/Photo Researchers/Getty Images; p. 6 Audrey Snider-Bell/Shutterstock.com; pp. 7, 13, 20 John Cancalosi/Photolibrary/Getty Images; p. 9 Bill Gorum/Flickr Open/Getty Images; p. 10 Joseph T Collins/Photo Researchers/Getty Images; p. 12 Joe McDonald/Visuals Unlimited/Getty Images; p. 15 Wild Horizon/Contributor/Getty Images; p. 16 JH Pete Carmichael/The Image Bank/Getty Images; p. 18 Rex Lisman/Flickr/Getty Images; p. 19 Paul Chesley/National Geographic/Getty Images; p. 21 (top) Suzanne L Collins/Photo Researchers/Getty Images; p. 21 (bottom) Gerold & Cynthia Merker/Visuals Unlimited/Getty Images; pp. 22 (left and middle) Matt Jeppson/Shutterstock.com; p. 22 Gary Meszaros/Visuals Unlimited/Getty Images.

Library of Congress Cataloging-in-Publication Data

Holmes, Parker, author.
    Amazing snakes of the Southwest and West coast / by Parker Holmes. — First edition.
        pages cm — (Amazing snakes)
    Includes index.
    ISBN 978-1-4777-6502-9 (library binding) — ISBN 978-1-4777-6503-6 (pbk.) — ISBN 978-1-4777-6506-7 (6-pack)
    1. Snakes—Southwestern States—Juvenile literature. 2. Snakes—Pacific Coast (U.S.)—Juvenile literature. I. Title.
    QL666.O6H757 2015
    597.96'0978—dc23
                                    2013044965

Manufactured in the United States of America

CPSIA Compliance Information: Batch #WS14PK6: For Further Information contact Rosen Publishing, New York, New York at 1-800-237-9932

Contents

Happy Snakes 4

Western Diamondback Rattlesnake 6

Coachwhip 8

Arizona Coral Snake 10

Common King Snake 12

Lyre Snake 14

Long-Nosed Snake 16

Sidewinder 18

Snake Country 20

Other Snakes in the Southwest
and West Coast 22

Glossary 23

Index 24

Websites 24

Happy Snakes

If you were a snake, where would you want to live? The sunny Southwest should be high on your list, and so should the West Coast state of California. They have the warm weather and natural **habitats** that make snakes very happy. Around 100 **species** of snakes, along with many other **subspecies**, live in these regions. That's a lot of snakes!

Most of these species are harmless. But this region is famous for its rattlesnakes. These **venomous** snakes are what many people call poisonous snakes. They're dangerous, so be careful if you hear rattlesnakes' rattling or buzzing! Are rattlesnakes your favorite snakes? Do you have another favorite kind? The Southwest and West Coast have a great selection of snakes, from deadly rattlesnakes to harmless little garter snakes. Let's take a look at some exciting snakes of the Southwest and West Coast!

The western diamondback rattlesnake, shown here, is a venomous snake. This deadly snake is common throughout the southwestern states and Mexico.

Western Diamondback Rattlesnake

The most famous snake in the Southwest is the western diamondback rattlesnake. This snake is **legendary**. It's a common snake in the Southwest, and it's also one of the most dangerous snakes in the country! The venom from a diamondback can be deadly to humans. The snakes use this venom to kill their food, mostly small mammals such as mice. Western diamondbacks are often between 3 and 5 feet (1–1.5 m) long. The record is 7.5 feet (2 m)! They're the second-biggest venomous snake in the country, behind eastern diamondbacks.

This western diamondback rattlesnake is in the middle of striking. Don't get too close! Their bites can be deadly.

Western diamondbacks are usually brown or gray with diamond-shaped patterns. These **reptiles** like to live in dry places, such as deserts, and can often be found hiding near rocks. Like most snakes, they want to be left alone. If they feel threatened, they'll shake the rattles on their tails as a warning to stay away. You should listen to their advice!

This western diamondback rattlesnake is eating a wood rat.

Coachwhip

The coachwhip is a snake with a fitting name. These snakes have long tails that are skinny and look braided, like whips. They were named after the whips used by **stagecoach** drivers in the old days. There are several subspecies of coachwhip snakes, and they come in a variety of colors. These slender snakes often grow to 4 or 5 feet (1.2–1.5 m). Coachwhips are related to the racer snake group, so they're really fast movers. These snakes are active daytime hunters. They'll eat lizards, insects, small mammals, and lots of different animals. They're not venomous, and they don't **constrict** their prey. Coachwhips just grab the food with their mouths and swallow it, often while it's still alive.

There's an old **folktale** about coachwhips that you shouldn't believe. The story goes that a coachwhip can wrap around your leg and whip you with its tail. That sounds kind of silly, doesn't it?

The red coachwhip can vary in color from pinkish to bright red.

Do you like rhymes? Here's a good one to remember, "Red touch yellow, kill a fellow; red touch black, friend of Jack." That will help you stay away from the Arizona coral snake. The coral snake is a venomous snake that has red, yellow, and black bands. These colors make it look similar to some harmless snakes. But on most harmless snakes, the red and black bands touch, while on coral snakes, the red and yellow touch.

Coral snakes have the most **toxic** venom of any snake in the country. But they're still not as dangerous as many Southwestern rattlesnakes. That's because the coral snake's mouth and fangs are so small that the snake doesn't deliver much venom. Also, they rarely try to bite people. They're shy snakes that like to hide during the day and come out at night. They're usually only 1 to 1.5 feet (31–46 cm) long.

The Arizona coral snake lives in northwestern Mexico as well as the southwestern United States.

Common King Snake

This reptile is called the king of snakes. There are several subspecies of the common king snake in the Southwest and on the West Coast. The California king snake, black desert king snake, and desert king snake all live here. Do you know why they have "king" in their names? It's because they **dominate** and eat other snakes, even venomous ones. The poison of venomous snakes doesn't kill them. King snakes are constrictors, so they squeeze their prey to death. Besides eating other snakes, king snakes eat a variety of small animals, such as mice and lizards.

This California king snake is eating a rattlesnake.

King snakes are often kept as pets because they are easy to care for and generally gentle.

The kind of common king snake you see most often in this region is the California king snake. It's typically between 2.5 and 4 feet (76–122 cm), and it's usually black with light bands. Many people think king snakes look attractive, so they've become popular pets. If handled gently, **tame** king snakes will often let you pick them up without biting you. Would you like to hold one?

Lyre Snake

The western lyre snake isn't considered a venomous snake. But don't tell that to a lizard! This snake produces a mild venom that isn't dangerous to humans, but it's strong enough to hurt its favorite food—lizards. A lyre snake has fangs in the back of its mouth instead of the front. That means it needs to chew on an animal before it can release any venom. Sometimes lyre snakes will also constrict their food.

Lyre snakes like to live in dry, rocky places. They're secretive snakes that usually come out only at night. They're brown or gray with darker blotches, and they usually grow to 2 or 3 feet (61–91 cm). They're called lyre snakes because they have marks on their heads that are shaped like lyres. A lyre is a musical instrument that was used in ancient Greece. It's kind of like a U-shaped harp.

This western lyre snake is slithering through a creosote bush. You can see the markings on its head that earned this snake its name.

Long-Nosed Snake

You won't see too many long-nosed snakes in the middle of the day. These shy, harmless snakes prefer to hunt at night. What's for supper? Lizards are at the top of the menu. Long-nosed snakes usually live in rocky deserts and prairies, where they can find plenty of lizards. During the day, these snakes often hide under rocks or in animal **burrows**.

You can guess why they're named long-nosed snakes. Their noses really are long and pointy. These snakes usually grow to between 1.5 and 2.5 feet (46–76 cm). They're often black, yellow, and red. These are the colors of the venomous coral snake. But coral snakes have colored bands that **encircle** their bodies, while long-nosed snakes have broken bands with blotches and specks. If you pick up a long-nosed snake, it probably won't bite. But things can get messy. It might squirt blood and poop from its tail. So watch out!

Sidewinder

If you're a snake, it's not easy to crawl on soft, hot sand. So the sidewinder rattlesnake has developed a great way to move across its desert habitat. It pushes its body sideways and kind of skips across the sand. This way, less of its belly has to touch the burning hot ground. This sideways motion also helps it move across sand that is soft and loose.

Here you can see how the sidewinder's coloring camouflages it in the sand.

The sidewinder is a type of rattlesnake. To find food, this venomous snake likes to **ambush** its prey. It will bury itself in the sand, wait for an animal to walk by, and then—surprise! A sidewinder's **camouflage** helps with the hunt. These snakes are usually tan or gray, so their colors help them blend in with the desert sand. Sidewinders often reach 1.5 to 2 feet (46–61 cm) long. They look like they have horns above their eyes, so some people call them horned rattlesnakes.

The sidewinder's unique way of moving leaves distinctive prints behind on the ground.

Snake Country

If you're looking for snakes in the Southwest and on the West Coast, you're in luck. This region has a great variety. They come in all different sizes and colors. You might find a big, hissing 6-foot (2 m) gopher snake. Or you might come across a tiny 6-inch (15 cm) sand snake. Some species, such as the desert night snake and rosy boa, can be hard to find. They usually come out only after dark.

This western patch-nosed snake is winding its way through a cactus in Arizona.

But other kinds, such as mountain patch-nosed snakes and garter snakes, aren't as secretive. They like to crawl around and hunt during the daytime.

Are you scared of snakes? The region has a lot of dangerous rattlesnakes. So you need to be careful. But remember that most species are harmless and are actually helpful. Snakes eat lots of pesky insects and rodents. Snakes are very interesting creatures, and the Southwest and West Coast are great places to find them. Snakes love it here!

The rosy boa is often found near rocky places. This slow-moving snake kills its prey by constricting it.

The checkered garter snake is a common, harmless snake found in the Southwest.

Other Snakes in the Southwest and West Coast

- Baird's rat snake
- Brazos water snake
- Broad-banded water snake
- California mountain king snake
- Flat-headed snake
- Milk snake
- Northern black-tailed rattlesnake
- Northern cat-eyed snake
- Northern green rat snake
- Organ pipe shovel-nosed snake
- Plains black-headed snake
- Plains slender blind snake
- Red diamond rattlesnake
- Regal black-striped snake
- Ridge-nosed rattlesnake
- Rock rattlesnake
- Saddled leaf-nosed snake
- Sharp-tailed snake
- Sonoran whipsnake
- Speckled rattlesnake
- Speckled racer
- Spotted leaf-nosed snake
- Striped racer
- Striped whipsnake
- Texas coral snake
- Thornscrub hook-nosed snake
- Tiger rattlesnake
- Twin-spotted rattlesnake
- Western black-headed snake
- Western ground snake
- Western pygmy rattlesnake
- Western shovel-nosed snake
- Western slender blind snake
- Yaqui black-headed snake

California mountain king snake

Western ground snake

Texas coral snake

Glossary

ambush (AM-bush) To attack by surprise from a hiding place.

burrows (BUR-ohz) Holes animals dig in the ground for shelter.

camouflage (KA-muh-flahj) A color or a pattern that matches the surroundings and helps hide something.

constrict (kun-STRIKT) To squeeze.

dominate (DAH-muh-nayt) To rule over or to stand out above all others.

encircle (in-SUR-kul) To form a circle around something.

folktale (FOHK-tayl) A story that has been handed down among people.

habitats (HA-buh-tats) The surroundings where animals or plants naturally live.

legendary (LEH-jen-der-ee) Very famous or well-known.

reptiles (REP-tylz) Cold-blooded animals with lungs and scales.

species (SPEE-sheez) A single kind of living thing. All people are one species.

stagecoach (STAYJ-kohch) A coach, pulled by a horse, that carried passengers and mail from stop to stop.

subspecies (SUB-spee-sheez) Types within a species.

tame (TAYM) Made gentle or raised by people.

toxic (TOK-sik) Poisonous.

venomous (VEH-nuh-mis) Having a poisonous bite.

Index

B
bands, 11, 13, 17

C
country, 6, 11

D
deserts, 7, 17

F
food, 6, 8, 14, 19

H
habitat(s), 4, 18
humans, 6, 14. See also people

M
mammals, 6, 8
mice, 6, 12

N
name(s), 8, 12

P
people, 4, 11, 13, 19. See also humans
prey, 8, 12, 19

R
rattlesnake(s), 4, 6, 11, 18–19, 21–22
reptile(s), 7, 12

rocks, 7, 17

S
species, 4, 20–21
subspecies, 4, 8, 12

T
tail(s), 7–8, 17
types, 19

V
venom, 6, 11, 14

W
warning, 7
weather, 4

Websites

Due to the changing nature of Internet links, PowerKids Press has developed an online list of websites related to the subject of this book. This site is updated regularly. Please use this link to access the list: www.powerkidslinks.com/amaz/swes/